A YOGA PARADE OF ANIMALS

A first fun picture book of yoga

By Pauline Mainland   Illustrated by Chris Perry

ELEMENT CHILDREN'S BOOKS

SHAFTESBURY, DORSET · BOSTON, MASSACHUSETTS · MELBOURNE, VICTORIA

rom a kneeling position sit back on your heels and place your hands by your knees. Start to breathe in deeply and at the same time tense your body, beginning with your feet, gradually working upwards. Don't forget to stretch and tense your hands and fingers, then look up at the ceiling and widen your eyes. Really feel like a lion waiting to spring on its prey. Give a big breath out, as you open your mouth wide, push your tongue out and downwards as far as it will go and listen to the sound of your breath coming out of your throat. Bring back your tongue, let go of the tension, and repeat twice more. The Lion is a very good posture for the throat area, and may help stop a cold which begins with a sore throat. It is said to help with bad breath and has been very useful helping people who stammer.

atha yoga is a system of physical and breathing exercises designed to bring together the physical and spiritual body. We breathe naturally all the time, but knowing how to breathe in a yoga way helps with many things in life. Hobbies like singing and swimming, and breathing difficulties that you get with asthma and bronchitis all really benefit from knowing how to work the breath.

▲ Breathe in, hands by knees stretch and tense the body beginning from the feet.

▲ Look up at ceiling, widen eyes, stick out tongue; breathe out through mouth, hear the sound in the throat.

▲ Bring back the tongue, let go of the tension, and repeat twice more.

Get into a lying position with your face down, bring your hands back to about chest level, elbows close into your body. Raise your head. Now make the tail by raising the head and lifting both legs and feet together a little way off the floor as you breathe in. Breathe out and then breathe normally as you move forward on your stomach keeping your legs straight, and using alternate hands push your body forward in a rolling movement, swaying your legs gently from side to side. Just imagine you're an alligator lumbering across the mud flats in search of prey.

This is known as a 'fun posture' and is not one of the classical yoga postures, but it helps the stomach and back muscles and is very funny but useful to do.

Breathing in yoga is divided into three areas known as low (tummy or Diaphragm) breath; middle (chest or Thoracic) breath; and upper (upper chest or Clavicular) breath. In the low breath, concentrate on watching the breath in the tummy area rising and falling.

▲ Lie face down, bring hands to chest level, elbows close to body.

▲ Raise head, keep both legs and feet together and lift.

▲ Use hands to push body forward, swaying legs from side to side, breathing normally.

From a standing position, breathe in and bring your arms high above your head. Breathe out, take your hands down to the floor, and walk your feet forward until your back is really stretched. Now, starting with a relaxed out breath, walk on all fours, moving your right arm and hand with the right leg and foot and then do the same with your left. If possible try not to bend your knees as you do the giraffe "walk"! Try to do this for a couple of minutes. This is another "fun posture" which stretches the back and the muscles at the back of the legs as well as strengthening the arms and the legs.

In the middle breath, your tummy is slightly drawn in and you focus the mind on your rib cage. Just watch the breath move and expand your ribs sideways, backwards, and upwards.

▶ Stand and breathe in, bring arms high above head.

▲ Breathe out, put hands on floor as far forward as possible, keep heels on floor, stretch the back.

▲ Walk on all fours moving right hand with right leg and left hand with left leg for 2 minutes, breathe freely.

Kneel down, leaving the tops of your feet flat on the floor, place your hands on your hips and push your hip and pelvic area forward, while leaning back a little from the waist. Then, place your right hand on the right foot, and your left hand on your left foot. (Tuck your toes under if this is difficult.) Allow your head to drop back. Breathe and relax into your chest area. Hold the position for a couple of breaths. Enjoy the arch of your back; it's like a camel's hump! This is a strong back bend so now kneel down and put your forehead on the floor, and rest your hands and arms at the sides of the body. This is called the Child posture. Rest for three breaths. Doing the Camel is excellent for anyone with chest problems like asthma and bronchitis because it opens wide the chest area.

▲ Kneel down, hip-width apart, place hands on hips. If it's difficult tuck your toes under.

▲ Lean back from waist and push hips and pelvis forward.

▲ Place a hand on each foot, arch back and hold for a couple of breaths. Relax in Child posture.

Child posture

In the upper chest breath, you can feel the breath extend up from the chest to the shoulders and bottom of the neck. When all three types of breath are joined together in one long breath, it is known as deep yoga breathing. It's knowing HOW to use the breath, and WHICH part to use in any "stressful" situation that makes doing yoga breathing so helpful in your everyday life.

Kneel down with knees a hip-width apart and hands and arms a shoulder-width apart, so that your hands, knees and feet are in a straight line. Breathe out very slowly through your mouth (hear the breath) and at the same time tuck in your chin and arch up your spine like a hump. Pause and count to three, then again very slowly as you breathe in through your nose, dip your spine down and lift up your head. Count to three with the breath held in, breathe out again, and as you do, tuck your chin in and arch your spine up again. Repeat five times. The Tiger is probably the most widely used posture in hospitals in India. It helps straighten the spine, drains the sinuses, rests the heart, and improves breathing and circulation. All the organs in the body drop into the right position in this posture. Really feel the strength and power of the tiger as you EXTEND the spine.

Yoga is a way of life dating back 6,000 years. At first there were only sitting postures for meditation, then the ancient Yogis studied animals, and found that by placing their bodies in similar positions, great benefits and strength came into the body.

▲ Kneel down, knees hip-width apart, hands shoulder-width apart, knees, hands, and feet all in a straight line.

▲ Breathe out through mouth, tuck in chin, arch up spine slowly. Hold for a count of three.

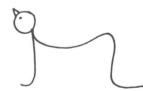

▲ Breathe in, dip spine down very slowly, lift up the head. Repeat 5 times.

Breathe in as you lie on the floor in a crooked-knee position, with legs and feet together and arms at the sides of your body. As you breathe out, make the sound of "sssssssss" and raise your back off the floor pushing it upwards towards the ceiling. Imagine you're a whale coming to the surface of the ocean and sending a great spray of water out of your spout. Hold the position for a few seconds, breathe in and gently return your back to the floor and repeat two or three times. Finish by curling the knees onto the chest. This posture strengthens the back and works the leg muscles, and the breathing really helps clear the lungs.

There are many different kinds of yoga and the one most widely practiced in the west is known as Hatha (pronounced Hat-ha). Ha relates to the sun, the male energy, and Tha relates to the moon, the female energy. We all have both energies and in Hatha yoga these are brought into balance for each of us, by using the breath and postures. Begin to notice what it means to be balanced in your everyday life, at play and at school.

▲ Lie down, knees and feet together, knees up, arms at the side.

▲ Breathe in and as you breathe out, make the sound of a ssss, raise the back off the floor. Hold for a count of three and breathe in, return back to floor. Repeat 3 times.

▲ Rest by curling knees onto chest.

Before trying this position, put a cushion on the floor in front of you, in case you fall over. From a squatting position, place your hands between your feet with your fingers spread out. Push the elbows into the insides of your knees, bring the weight onto your hands, lift up your head, and raise your feet from the ground. Hold for a few seconds and breathe freely. You are just like a bird waiting very quietly and determinedly for a worm to appear. The Blackbird posture improves balance and concentration. The two go together; you can't balance without concentration. It also strengthens your hands, wrists and arms.

Once the physical body is controlled, it is possible to start work on the mind. The mind can be just like a naughty puppy chasing its tail, or a monkey jumping from branch to branch, never settling anywhere. Body and mind can be controlled by concentrating on one thing at a time, and gradually the mind will become calm and quiet.

▲ Get cushion!

▲ Squat down, put hands between feet, fingers spread, push elbows into inside of knees.

▲ Bring the weight onto hands, lift up head, and raise feet. Hold for a count of three. Breathe freely.

Standing upright with legs and feet together, breathe in, and as you breathe out, bend your left knee and clasp your left foot close into your body with your left hand. Breathe in and raise your right arm above your head, breathe out, then breathe freely, concentrating on the feeling of balance. Now repeat on the other side. This is another balance posture which takes concentration to perform. It also strengthens the legs, and keeps the spine straight.

Remember that when you balance the physical body it affects everything, including your mind and emotions, not just when you are doing the yoga positions but as you go about your everyday life — playing, eating, sleeping. The positions help to develop a strong "inner strength." In yoga terms this is called Atman. Some people might call it "the force!" The body in yoga is known as the Temple of the Spirit, so it is important to look after it well.

▷ Stand upright, legs and feet together. Breathe in.

▷ Breathe out, bend left knee, and hold left foot close to body with left hand.

▷ Breathe in, raise right arm above head, breathe out, hold the position, breathe freely for a couple of minutes. Repeat on other side.

This is probably one of the most "knotted" positions in yoga. From a standing position, bring your right leg over your left thigh, just above the knee, and rest the back of your right thigh on the front of your left thigh. Bend your elbows, bringing your arms to chest height. Rest your left elbow on the front of your right upper arm, near the elbow joint. Bring the back of your right hand into the palm of your left, curling your fingers over the right. Rest your chin on your hands, and lower your elbows onto your knees. Fix your eyes on a point – like an eagle fixing its gaze on its prey. Hold the position for a few seconds, breathing freely. Relax! Don't grip! Release, come back to standing pose, and repeat on the other side putting the left leg over the right and the right elbow over the left arm. The Eagle develops the ankle and calf muscles and removes stiffness in the shoulders as well as developing concentration on one point.

In yoga, it is said that the more "knotted" the body is in a posture, the calmer the mind becomes. This is turn affects the nervous system of the body. The more yoga you do, the quieter and calmer you become.

Stand up, bend the knees slightly, bring right leg over left thigh, above the knee.

Rest right thigh on front of left thigh. Rest left elbow on front of right upper arm.

Place back of right hand into palm of left, curling fingers over the right, rest chin on hands and lower elbows to knees. Hold for 3 seconds. Breathe freely. Repeat on other side.

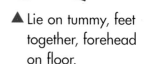

ie on your tummy, feet together, forehead on the floor. Bring your hands close to the sides of your chest and bend your elbows. Breathe out, tuck in your chin, and look down towards your chest. As you breathe in, very slowly, brush your mat with your nose, mouth, and chin and raise your head off the floor. Look up at the ceiling, breathe out, and hold the position for a few seconds, breathing normally. Breathe in, then slowly come back down, breathing out as you go, brushing the mat with your chin, mouth, and nose and again looking towards your chest. Relax with your face down before repeating and then do the Child posture to ease your back. The Cobra increases the flexibility of the spine, strengthens the arms and hands, opens the throat (very helpful for sore throats), and aids the removal of poisons from the kidneys.

▲ Lie on tummy, feet together, forehead on floor.

▲ Bring hands close to side of chest, bend elbows. Breathe out, tuck chin in; breathe in, slowly brush mat with nose, mouth, chin, as the head, shoulders, upper back are raised off the floor.

▲ Look up at ceiling, breathe out, hold for few seconds. Breathe in, breathe out and slowly come back down. Repeat. Do Child posture.

ill-power, or the power to will something, is one of the most important benefits from yoga, giving us single-minded determination to succeed in whatever we become involved in. If the will is strong the mind is strong, and if the mind is strong, it can strengthen the will. A little phrase that is worth repeating is: "I can, I will, I am, AND I am, I will, I can." This will help remove doubts, fears and negativity.

itting back on the heels, put your arms behind your back and clasp one hand around your other wrist. Breathe in, then as you come forward to place your forehead on the floor, breathe out and chant the Bee mantra "mmmmmmmmmmmmm." Remain in the position a few seconds, breathe in as you return to the upright position, then repeat four or five times more.

antra yoga is the yoga of sound, and is a form of meditation which physically vibrates the body, rather like tuning a piano. The most important mantra of all is "OM," which is known as the sound of the universe. OM is split into A-U-M. The A sound comes from the back of the throat and vibrates

from the toes to the tummy, the U sound comes through the mouth and vibrates from the tummy to the throat, and the M sound is felt on the closed lips and vibrates from the throat to the top of the head. Bhamari, or the Black Bee mantra, is made the same as the M sound of OM.

▲ Sit back on heels.

▲ Put arms behind the back, clasp one hand around the other wrist.

▲ Breathe in, come forward slowly, place forehead on floor and as you breathe out chant mmmmmmmm. Stay down for a few seconds, breathe in and come up slowly. Repeat 5 times.

In a kneeling position, spread your knees as far apart as comfortable, keeping your toes touching behind you. Bring the first finger and thumb together on each hand (this keeps the energy within) and place your hands on your knees. In the Frog, concentration is on the low breath. Feel the rise and fall of the tummy area as you breathe in and out. Find the quietness in this peaceful pose. Just watch the breath. Enjoy the stillness.

To meditate is "to empty one's mind of thoughts." We listen to what our inner being is telling us. We learn to quieten the never-ending, jumping "monkey" mind and are able to concentrate on whatever we do in life. It calms us down, and makes us aware of "the force" within.

▲ Kneel with knees spread wide, keep big toes touching.

▲ Bring first finger and thumb together.

▲ Breathe quietly for a few minutes and feel the rise and fall of the tummy area in the Diaphragm breath.

SLEEPING SNAKE

You can do this with as many of your friends or family as you can fit into a room. First decide who is to be the "head" and who is to be the "tail." The "head" lies down in a crook-knee position, closes his or her eyes and focuses breathing in the tummy, just watching it rise and fall. Then he or she chooses a second person who lies down in the same way, but rests his or her head on the "head's" tummy. The second person tunes into the "head's" rhythm of breathing, conscious of sharing the experience with someone else. The second person chooses a third and so on, until everybody is involved, the "tail" being the last. Keep the breath in tune throughout the snake. This lovely position links your group together in a state of complete relaxation and a feeling of being at one with everybody and everything.

R elaxation is a vital part of yoga. True relaxation is a re-creation of our whole being, mind, emotions, and body. It is a state where healing can take place. Through yoga and particularly the Sleeping Snake we can learn that there is a togetherness with all life. That feeling of unity with all, quietness, and stillness is something to work towards in everything you do.

▲ The "head" lies down in crooked-knee position, eyes closed, breathe from the tummy. 2nd person lies down in same position with head on "head's" tummy. Listen to the rhythm of the breathing.

▲ 3rd person does the same, and so on. The whole snake needs to breathe together. Relax. Peace.